eventide

eventide

Poems by

Sally Stewart Mohney

© 2020 Sally Stewart Mohney. All rights reserved.
This material may not be reproduced in any form, published,
reprinted, recorded, performed, broadcast,
rewritten or redistributed without
the explicit permission of Sally Stewart Mohney.
All such actions are strictly prohibited by law.

Cover design by Shay Culligan
Cover image, "Blue Horizon," courtesy of Frances Roosevelt

ISBN: 978-1-952326-50-9

Kelsay Books
502 South 1040 East, A-119
American Fork, Utah, 84003

for my family
for my river

Acknowledgments

I'm grateful to be included in the following:

Broad River Review: "Fonta Flora remains," Ron Rash Poetry Award Finalist

Fourth & Sycamore: "Rules for the dead," "The summer we read Dostoyevsky"

Georgia Poetry Society Reach of Song Anthology: "Appling County Breach," "Upcountry, hard water"

James Dickey Review: "king tide"

Noctua Review: "Under the old trestle, Telfair County"

North Carolina Literary Review: "In your Mother's foothills," James Applewhite Poetry Prize Honorable Mention, "Jackson from the Third Floor," James Applewhite Poetry Prize Finalist

POEM: "Off the North Sea"

San Pedro River Review: "Sleeping with the TV on"

Waccamaw: "Birthing the Room"

I particularly want to thank Karen Kelsay and Shay Culligan of Kelsay Books for this gift.

I'm honored to have Frances Roosevelt's beautiful painting grace the cover.

A special thanks to the Whitfields for all of their work for the North Carolina Foothills Conservancy.

For my poetry families, with thanksgiving.

Contents

William's wake	11
king tide	13
In the wake of	14
The summer we read Dostoyevsky	15
Sleeping with the TV on	16
Under the old trestle outside Eastman, Telfair County	17
Jackson, from the third floor	19
Appling County Breach	21
Fonta Flora remains	22
In your Mother's foothills	24
winter's tide	25
Upcountry, hard water	26
nine secrets the mountain did not tell you	28
Off the North Sea	29
Landscape with your Mother's Omens	30
Still Life with Mother's Totems	32
Rules for the dead	33
Birthing the room	34
Flood Street, SW3	35
What endures?	36
Your May darkness	37
Voice from the field	38
seed creek christening	40
by the first pond in the third wood	41

William's wake

i. Imagine a spring stratus stack—
    the height of the Andes—under a pale
    rogue sun. Gather the smell

    of sour
    rain from the back dune,
    wet live oaks, salt-pruned—

    resin up to the rales.

ii. Think,
    Canopy of winged wax
    trees—now beach
    burnt pilgrims, blue—
    swamped.

iii. Capture the calm cowl of wind
     in the Lean
     Afternoon, tide
     culls cast quartz,
     entombs: white bird

     under lit—pickled
     black stare.

iv. Beneath a moth
    halo moon, may you grow Still
    Enough,
    even as runnels decant
    blue shadows
    in drowned embayments,

Let the slant silvered jetty—
grant a blistered sanctuary.

v. Witness

wick of smoked black
oak, as it speaks:

one bare tree
& one white bird

king tide

When cormorants perch on warning
poles and cloud-white
waves breach the sea wall—
flooding the ocean forest—
there is a tacit leaf of sadness.

When a horseshoe skull lands on hard &
bitter sand—copper bowl
tide-upturned, lost. Stranded sand dollars—cool

as stones. Still white salmon in bone sanctuary, blind
to: sky moths/dusk thoughts—disquiet
clad in silk air, stray
shadows coalesce   as hallowing gray   solace.
Steel light becomes one lost cloud—an ether portal
with a charcoal rain edge.

Until the mist
as silent silver totem
as one gray glove
as imaginary saint—gives way

to the hunter's moon

In the wake of

contrail clouds
culling through
the black
and white photograph

of you, your brother
and the dog

on the old beach.

Steel-thunder rales—
winter-blue. Strike

lifts your tow-colored hair,
you cradle your brother's dark nape just so—

as his starfish
hand clasps
his dog's skull—
sepia spaces
between each
finger.

Cold pale sea
in the background

with a few, possible
spindly oats, taxed

for sunlight. Soon
sea smoke, no
salt-wind, no sky

seeded stars

The summer we read Dostoyevsky

I don't remember anyone else but you.

First you were lost in Oates' wonderland
then you joined me in crime
& punishment

in the belly of that gray
shingle motel on Pawleys Island.

Evenings we rose from the depths
sat at the hunt board to peel shrimp on newspaper,
bit into blood ripe tomatoes.

Didn't we lie in the sun with olive oil over our slim brown limbs?

Then back to our hidden quarters to perch on rusty cots
to muse over Siddhartha between Raskolnikov pages—

crickets in the corners of the knotty pine cave—

our own small ship—even though
we were well below deck.

I am with your ghost again

Sleeping with the TV on

in that yellow motel
in west Monroe.

Silent reflex: reach for your small
dog—the blanket furrow
at your knee. Absent,

screen still casts
aprons of glow.

Unwilling to host
your parents'
ghosts
alone.

One-inch throw-bolt
thrown.

Outside the escape window
dark arms of white ash
brace.

Under the old trestle
outside Eastman, Telfair County

Corroded swing-bridge—
warren & truss. Rust-colored
beech trees. Lone banked raft.
No boats pass under
the tower shed.

I happen upon you—

& you turn to look at me
as if you are the last man
on earth, and you are—
poised
on the brink
but can't bear
to stay—still
that blue cotton
shirttail, faded
denims. Your pale
feet in our forgotten
river
bed.

There are too many sudden
bright bulbs
that surge up
every March.

For seventeen years,
   why have you hidden?

Then I realize what I've known all along:
alone by the water
is where you belong.

You aren't the only one who
can turn into ether—

now it's my turn to haunt you

Jackson, from the third floor

casement, cottoned
with dead bees—
the sky—
a long exposure. High
summer, shank of day.

Yellowed downtown
yearns to sip canopied
shade. Rusted arches

encrusted with weeping
fig. Cast street lamps,
bleached baseball
field. Hospital block,
bank block, bistered
Travel Lodge. Dollar

store/pawn shop/tires &
batteries. Flint Furniture, Lost
Brothers Machine Shop
hunch in sepia spill under

water tower. Past
East Pascagoula—

the Pearl River—first a silver
fissure, later a fulvous
flame. Blazing white quarry.

Bus chunters
past, full of hollow-eyed
passengers—under
cadged cadmium
light

loneliness draws a picture on your back

Appling County Breach

Battened barns, on bitten
orange shoulders. Black

tumbled letters on forgotten
marquee. Shackled
superette. Rust-awninged
windows. Earth-brick Pentecostal
church shaded by bearded trees.

Vacant ladderbacks on still porches.

Ladled lakes circled by live oak
scrim. Branches, in first gust, lift
over runneled acres. Steel echo
of warblers—from bitumen

to riverine. Wood duck lift
from hard pond water. Wimpled
magnolias shield Cooper's
hawk, as calming hood. Violet hole
opens from bowl of sky. Creek

cattle collect in charged
chambers between pecan stanchions,
face spring's fractured spur.

Fonta Flora remains

*Fonta Flora was a village in western Burke County,
North Carolina, that was flooded in 1918 to create Lake James.*

The sower sleeps—
moored to an iron
bed. The small of his back
the smell of striped gin
the sound of a screen door closing.

Under the lone cypress, the well
tastes like river rock.

In an orchard mile:
shadowless white barn/
corn/sugar beet/black
earth. No time to till. Only
seed tick, wire grass.

Tide threads the black gorge
then rips, reams, submerges
the valley road, swallows
the hopyard. Wake portaging

chimney/tractor/chapel
alders & willows/ kerosene
lamp, a train car.

Upmountain, shoals from a low
and quiet creek
seek the geese, who flew
to wait in the covered bridge.

Where are the bank swallows?
Where are the shallows?

one silver ghost in one blue farm

In your Mother's foothills

by the fourth blue river,
in the seventh woods,

you are covered
by a fine mat of ash
leaves. Warm
wraith
nest-nettled
under vested valley floor.

Wood thrush next

to your right ear—
a feathered flag. Your feet soon

bloom pale. Eyelids, pink
sepals. Fungus threads
rhizomed hair while unmoored

limbs decay: mineral

white-bladed beauty
in salmon-colored
clay. Blue shadows of winged elm
leave bars on new snow.

Ooh nay thla nah, hee oo way gee*

*Amazing Grace, Cherokee version

winter's tide

i. west of january
yoked yew trees—

color of old snow—

one with a cane
shrouded
in field-borne
smoke

ii. offers dark birds
bent towards late solstice

iii. her brindle branches rake
clouds cloaked
in gray solace

fog-chilled
moon-pulled

how many lanterns are left?

Upcountry, hard water

I.

Train chunters past
three horses—
Wyeth white—
up pasture. Orchard,
rusted.

II.

Horses—now lung gray—
nose bitter grounds. In waxed
coat, fawn hood
you unlatch
the stone gate—
your hands cold
holly leaves. Split
rail fence heaves. Dead
water oak—sawed off shotgun
18 degrees.

III.

Snow-cemmed house—tucked
dormers, chimney pot.
Spilled suet. Orphan
barrow of boat paint.
In the limestone
alcove, a hectoring
cane. Hung musquatch coat.

His patina kettle boils.
Proven bread & pilchard
pie. Blood pudding. Deer
dinner on pewter charger—
tooth crack—

embedded buckshot

nine secrets the mountain did not tell you

cloud fall beguiles silver
withers of the mountain

barren wind saint, fell-field
fogbreak   winter teeth find

budwood, white
bark candlestick

fall line: snow sewn in half
goat stitched into the earth

gray salt barn
heather rests like sheep

canted moon
false nimbus

forsake the cold harbor, forsake the fugue

just enough hemlock

Off the North Sea

In the dark country, the black
estuary is still as you skim the vast
satin surface. Mountains hang
above—cirrus blue, mute.

Deep into the wake
of evergreen arms, lichen
coves unfold. Gray rocks bleed
green over glazed water.

One dry waterfall—now
a mercury thread—leads
to a tumbled tide—
a sanctuary of stone.

A feeling of a cold pasture
paling between two peaks:

lighthouse strikes a rust barn—
another ochre with a sod roof—

then turns away.

Landscape with your Mother's Omens

Winter, without her

i. Trapped inside January—

unsent bird waits
on the ash branch.

White hart
stands on the other side
of the footbridge.

Drowned brook
broken under a sturgeon moon—

the world disappears in front of you.

ii. March land

What draws you to this place,
this boundary between realms?
Hunting lonesome spoor
to keep yourself company.

Linen air pulls
a skein of clouds.

What stands behind the sky?

iii. Solstice light

quickening through shawled oaks
wraps a poultice around you.

Egrets—scraps of white paper—
lift, float.

the least tern tolls the recanted hour

Still Life with Mother's Totems

A rock from a walk, glass bowl
from a dance. Silver anniversary
plate reflects matches from the club. Your
father's Old-Fashioned glass. White
conch, shellacked horn, curdled
Christmas candles, a brittle corsage.

Small hickory box turned
from a childhood tree—*her sheltering
spot.* Inside, one starling husk.

Yolky polaroid labeled 'Aix'
in magic marker: limestone
hearth, creamy clay
pitcher. She pours, toasts, drinks.

Leaning closer, she smiles, as you
harken back. Her mind now
reachable
only

by ferry.

Rules for the dead

in your dream—

the old house is lit and no one
is home. You slip in—a stranger now—
but somehow it feels like the old comfort:
whitewashed brick floor, iron lantern.

A yellowed corridor afternoon. The sliding
glass door leads to the garden where soon

the dead alight: your mother and father
come to roost. The weight of the unspoken.

Your mother has a hazel gaze and holds
her dark purse in her lap—
the size of a king salmon—
with a gold clasp. Your father's
cypress-gray face wreathed
with woe.

You are on tenterhooks—
because if you speak—

they will suddenly fade
like fog. How do they enter
and then leave
this old world
so seamlessly? Now
no one home

except you

Birthing the room

Open bellows
bloom birch beams. Pump
cottonwood stain, spin linen
slips, varnish raffia. Mill

walnut planks, cedar shiplap.
Shake the soffit, prime the doors.
Sheath the windows in pewter
nimbus & wool skein. Hone

the lace white, blow mercury
lamp, glass beaker. Wire holes,
trim bulbs. Polish nickel knobs,
pulls poised. Silent

oiled bronze levers—keyed,
bolted. Eyebrows at the back
gable, seal the flat-felled seam.

Flood Street, SW3

*bitterns land to gather
on the black embankment*

Crossing the bridge: the horse
guards. She senses the clack
cadence before
she draws back

floor to ceiling sheers—
spies the gold helmets,
red jackets, black
horses nodding

in step under
steep elm clouds. When she
unlocks the casement,
the balcony—now rife
with bougainvillea—

ponders. In silk air,
sage rain trembles
over the bowers.

She sets a gray
fire and swallows
cake bread. Her pale feet
rise in the porcelain tub
on the herringbone floor.

The dogwood-white limbus
of her eye. Mute swan—

mist rises off of her—nothing
left but a cage of feather & twine.

What endures?

Not your lonely lost
train
of thought—

now a stray
frayed second
self,
moving
through your mind:

a gray ghost
limned within
the deep sea

of your memory—

a dim decanted
tide of grief.

Your May darkness

Light from the terrace:

the one bud, the one
bird.

That plow of cedar—
the familiar column of shadow—
under one lost
mountain.

Near the bank—
a reflection of magnolia
goblets—white-gloved,
upright—as deer
browse
in borrowed light.

Outfall twilight:

a night cereus waxes
a white torch
in her throat—
the corolla's ceiling—

then disappears.

you may never
understand this lake

Voice from the field

Wind—that wandering
saint—amongst a congregation
of clouds. Soon the woods
arrive—staunch
in their elmness.

How old creek longs to speak.
How its groundwater—blood-
warm, pasture-born—yearns
for a tide, a swell—to host
scores of swaying trout.

Its water will never know the peace
of a lake, instead presses
a clutch of maple leaves
against its cider heart. Broken
stones shield olive
cottonmouth, pickerel
sheaves. Hickory hulls
litter its belly. How it hungers

to be a river—flashing
chilled silver depths
to the sea—ferrying
flocks of boats and birds.
Fears being
a dry ravine—blinded
by paper-white birch. Old

creek peers up at gray
fox as she sips—
tastes the river-pull
of flint
in her mouth. The sky—

still—
a great reach

of blue.

seed creek christening

cantering cloud reef   late sun stains
sudden cataract   whets rim to dam

salt-white birch   fir ranks wake, forget
wintering weathercock   atop crib barn

wild goat   alpaca   then canted cow

lone roe deer ferries across winding hazel water
bank to bank   vaults shore
runnel rises   shakes snow fleece   courses

fathoms, from an old map
plumbs a luminous deepening

channels roam through   loam/peat/leaves
candent waves seep   sow yellow clearing

seek watermark

by the first pond in the third wood

the sound of water   horses in the rain   white horses

among dark pecan stanchions   drifting down to drink

green water under gold maples   fawn shoulders   wild

magnolia   white gate   purple martins   roan cloud

listen like a lake

About the Author

Sally Stewart Mohney's poetry collection, *Low Country, High Water,* (Texas Review Press) won the Southern Poetry Anthology Prize: North Carolina. Other publications include *A Piece of Calm,* (Finishing Line Press) and *pale blue mercy,* (Main Street Rag, Author's Choice Series).

Her work has appeared in the *Charlotte Observer, Cortland Review, Iodine Poetry, Town Creek Poetry, Verse Daily, WinningWriters.com* and anthologies such as *Reach of Song, Southern Poetry Anthology Volume VII, Stone, River, Sky* and elsewhere.

She is the recipient of the Jesse Rehder Writing Prize from the University of North Carolina in Chapel Hill.

She lives a thousand feet from the Chattahoochee River.

www.ingramcontent.com/pod-product-compliance
Lightning Source LLC
Chambersburg PA
CBHW071641090426
42738CB00013B/3180